LIGHTNING BOLT BOOKS™

Dangerous Hurricanes

Lola Schaefer

Lerner Publications • Minneapolis

Thank you,
Jason Thistlethwaite,
University of
Waterloo

Lerner Publications Company
An imprint of Lerner Publishing Group, Inc.
241 First Avenue North
Minneapolis, MN 55401 USA

For reading levels and more information, look up this title at www.lernerbooks.com.

Main body text set in Billy Infant Regular. Typeface provided by SparkType.

Library of Congress Cataloging-in-Publication Data

Names: Schaefer, Lola M., 1950- author.
Title: Dangerous hurricanes / Lola Schaefer.
Description: Minneapolis : Lerner Publications, [2022] | Series: Lightning bolt books—earth in danger | Includes bibliographical references and index. | Audience: Ages 6-9 | Audience: Grades 2-3 | Summary: "Hurricanes are big storms that can cause a lot of damage. Discover how a hurricane forms and the conditions that can make one worse as well as how to stay safe in a hurricane"—Provided by publisher.
Identifiers: LCCN 2021018540 (print) | LCCN 2021018541 (ebook) | ISBN 9781728441405 (library binding) | ISBN 9781728447957 (paperback) | ISBN 9781728444840 (ebook)
Subjects: LCSH: Hurricanes—Juvenile literature.
Classification: LCC QC944.2 .S34 2022 (print) | LCC QC944.2 (ebook) | DDC 551.55/2—dc23

LC record available at https://lccn.loc.gov/2021018540
LC ebook record available at https://lccn.loc.gov/2021018541

Manufactured in the United States of America
1-49911-49754-8/2/2021

Table of Contents

Hurricanes Destroy!

Ocean waves rise higher and higher. The wind blows faster and harder. Waves crash onshore.

Rain pounds roofs. Power lines fall. Ocean water tears apart homes and schools. A hurricane destroys.

Hurricanes can create dangerous winds, rain, and flooding.

Hurricanes often form near the equator, the invisible line around the middle of Earth.

A hurricane is a large, tropical storm that forms over warm ocean water. Its center, called an eye, is a low-pressure zone.

The eyewall surrounds the eye. It has the storm's hardest rain and strongest winds. Past the eyewall are rainbands that turn around the eye.

The eyewall is the most dangerous part of a hurricane.

How Hurricanes Begin

Hurricanes form when warm, wet air over water begins to rise. Cooler air drops down to where the warm air was.

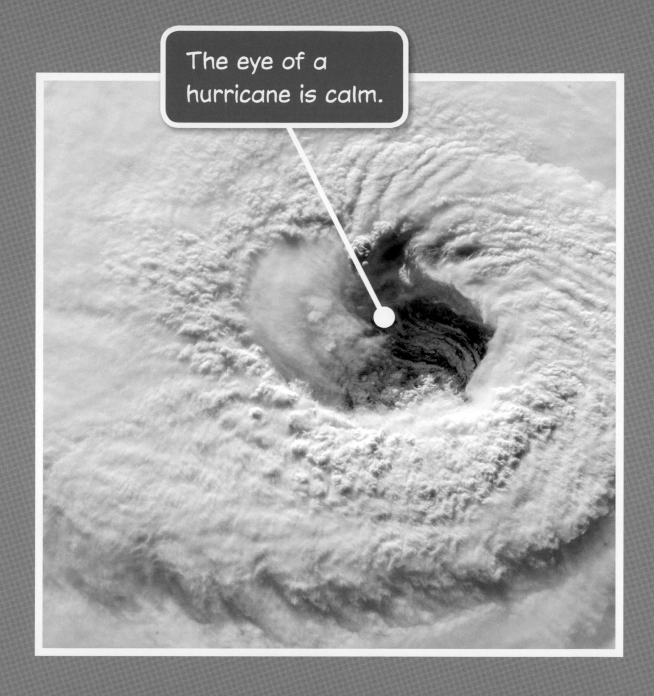

Clouds and thunderstorms form. They grow bigger and begin to circle the hurricane's eye.

A hurricane destroyed this walkway.

The warmer the ocean, the more energy a hurricane has. With more energy, the hurricane is bigger and does more damage.

Climate change warms oceans. It also melts sea ice and raises ocean levels. Coastlines will shrink, and stronger hurricanes will form.

Rising seas and stronger hurricanes will put coastal homes in more danger.

Dangerous Hurricanes

Most hurricanes stay over the oceans and do no damage. But when they come ashore, they can destroy buildings and hurt people.

This hurricane's winds blew as fast as 155 miles (250 km) per hour.

Hurricane winds can blow 75 to 160 miles (121 to 257 km) per hour. They can uproot trees, pick up cars, and even tear buildings apart. High winds push tall waves onto the shore.

Hurricane Alex flooded streets in Portugal in 2016.

During a hurricane, seawater rises. This storm surge slams onto land. It can flood roads and towns 20 to 30 miles (32 to 48 km) inland.

Hurricanes are dangerous for people and animals. They can lose their homes or get trapped by high water. Sometimes they get hurt or drown.

Floodwaters may have strong, invisible currents that can be dangerous.

Staying Safe

Scientists follow tropical storms. They predict when and where hurricanes will form. They track storm paths and give warnings.

An emergency kit should contain only food that won't spoil.

If you live near the coast, keep extra food and water in your home. Pack an emergency kit. Listen to weather updates.

Boarding up windows can prevent the glass from breaking.

If a hurricane comes near you, board up windows. Bring pets inside. If asked to evacuate your home, stay away until the danger has passed.

Hurricanes are part of nature. We cannot prevent them, but we can be prepared. Having a plan can help you stay safe.

Make a hurricane safety plan with your family!

I Survived a Hurricane

On August 3, 2020, Hurricane Isaias came ashore in North Carolina. Oak Island fire chief Chris Anselmo watched large waves form on the ocean. A storm surge of 6 to 8 feet (1.8 to 2.4 m) of water tore away at docks, stairways, and decks. Heavy winds and rains brought down power lines. Anselmo survived and so did Oak Island.

Hurricane Facts

- Hurricanes are placed in five categories based on wind speed. Category 5 hurricanes have the highest wind speeds and are the most destructive.

- Hurricanes turn counterclockwise in the Northern Hemisphere and clockwise in the Southern Hemisphere.

- The wettest hurricane on record is Hurricane Harvey in 2017. Over six days, Harvey dropped 27 trillion gallons (102 trillion L) of water over parts of Texas and Louisiana.

Glossary

climate change: long-term changes in global temperature due to human and natural activity

coastline: the place where the land and the ocean meet

evacuate: to move away from an area because it is dangerous

prevent: to stop something from happening

storm surge: when the sea rises because of a storm

tropical: having to do with the hot and humid climate

Learn More

Britannica Kids: Tropical Cyclone
https://kids.britannica.com/kids/article/tropical-cyclone/390127

Kim, Carol. *Dangerous Floods*. Minneapolis: Lerner Publications, 2022.

National Geographic Kids: Hurricane
https://kids.nationalgeographic.com/science/article/hurricane

Rathburn, Betsy. *Hurricanes*. Minneapolis: Bellwether, 2020.

Rivera, Andrea. *Hurricanes.* Minneapolis: Abdo Zoom, 2018.

Weather Wiz Kids: Hurricanes
https://www.weatherwizkids.com/weather-hurricane.htm

Index

Photo Acknowledgments

Image credits: Leighton Collins/Shutterstock.com, p. 4; FotoKina/Shutterstock.com, p. 5; Nejron Photo/Shutterstock.com, p. 6; NASA, pp. 7, 9; Carl & Ann Purcell/Getty Images, p. 8; john harding photography/Getty Images, p. 10; AmbientShoot/Shutterstock.com, p. 11; Mike Phillips/Shutterstock.com, p. 12; Tony Arruza/Getty Images, p. 13; Rui Caria/Getty Images, p. 14; johnmoorefour/Shutterstock.com, p. 15; Fineart1/Shutterstock.com, p. 16; skodonnell/Getty Images, p. 17; Prentiss Findlay/Shutterstock.com, p. 18; pkline/Getty Images, p. 19.

Cover image: NASA/Terra > MODIS.